B. CONSERVATIVE

*"In this present crisis,
government is not the solution to our problem,
government is the problem."*

–**Ronald Reagan**

Copyright 2018

ONSERVATIVE

Billy the elephant loves the American Constitution

Because he believes the founding fathers have the right solution

But Suzie and other donkeys believe freedom is oppressive

So they made their own leftist society, and it's quite far from progressive

So follow Billy and Suzie's lives but don't be surprised

That the left's agenda is simply idiocy disguised

B. CONSERVATIVE

B. CONSERVATIVE

Suzie's goverment mandates public schooling, quite profusely

And everyone suffers there, including poor Suzie

The classrooms are too small

The playground has just one ball

Teachers jaded by tenure just don't seem to care

And with meager materials, every student must share

Books and supplies grow more outdated each year

Why won't the state help them? Well, that's not quite clear

B. CONSERVATIVE

B. CONSERVATIVE

For Billy there are both public and charter schools

Where people are able to get all the right tools

Classrooms are just the right size

So teachers help them get wise

And in this system, no child is left behind

However some say charter schools are unrefined

"They use up tax dollars for the public institution!"

But is leaving kids in bad schools any solution?

B. CONSERVATIVE

B. CONSERVATIVE

Oh no! What's this?

Billy and Suzie have the same sickness

In Suzie's world, Doctors can't have a business

Because earning a profit is deemed malicious

So to one common doctor, Suzie must go

And wait in a long line with that much more woe

It's not strange that the quality of care is so low

Mainly because no competition remains the status quo

B. CONSERVATIVE

B. CONSERVATIVE

Billy, however, knew he was in good hands

Because doctors compete to be best in the land

So Billy went and gave the doctor his pay

And was cured of sickness hip-hip, hooray!

Great healthcare, you see, can never truly be free

Someone has to pay the doctor, and that's either you or me

So it's better to have supply and demand agree

And let the free market decide where that should be

B. CONSERVATIVE

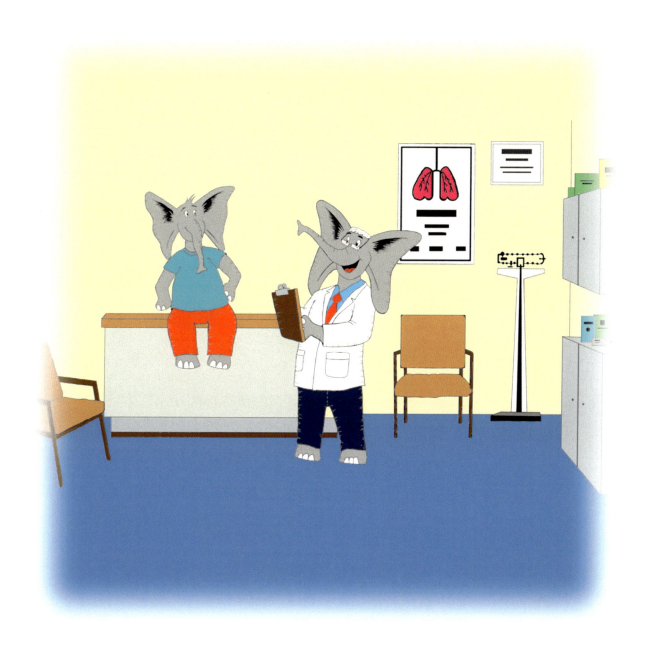

B. CONSERVATIVE

Time has passed, and Billy and Suzie are now in college

But there's something Suzie finds hard to acknowledge

She finds that other people's opinions can be quite pensive

And wondered, "Don't they realize I find that offensive?"

So Suzie gathered friends and they yelled in a loud burst,

"Stop speaking now and put our feelings first!

These microaggressions are societal transgressions

It doesn't matter the expression – it's all oppression!"

B. CONSERVATIVE

B. CONSERVATIVE

Even at Billy's college, free speech is a debate

Billy argues, "Remember what our constitution advocates!

How can censorship be a form of progression?

If we eliminate our freedoms, then that's regression!"

Life has a lot of sensitive topics, that's for sure!

But if we act on emotion, then we can never mature

So open your ears and hear what folks have to say

You might be surprised to learn something new today!

B. CONSERVATIVE

B. CONSERVATIVE

Being a grown-up means you have to do more and that's not easy

But Suzie will learn that more government can make you queasy

Suzie works hard in society, a job is an economic maker!

But doesn't realize that their government is just full of takers

"Why isn't my handout more? I need to make ends meet!

I need more than just the food I eat!"

B. CONSERVATIVE

B. CONSERVATIVE

So Suzie grabbed a sign and demanded to be paid more,

"If government doesn't increase salaries, then this is war!"

So the government shrugged and increased the pay rates

However, business couldn't afford all these new mandates

So employers laid off workers and Suzie was filled with rage

The standard of living doesn't rise with the minimum wage

B. CONSERVATIVE

B. CONSERVATIVE

But Billy starts his own company and wants it to thrive

Free enterprise is a vehicle that puts the economy in drive

A business employs people and making money is a must

But to confuse profits with sales is simply unjust!

B. CONSERVATIVE

B. CONSERVATIVE

Billy needs to buy supplies, pay employees and the rent

And in the first year of business, he hardly made a cent

But when Billy paid himself and had a good feeling in his gut

Here come the leftists, demanding their cut

B. CONSERVATIVE

B. CONSERVATIVE

From the start, you see, Suzie just had it rough

It's because society didn't value freedom enough

Suzie's government check just isn't that much

Bad things happen when the government is a crutch

So people will march and claim the State is a charity,

"You have to give us more!" they'll say with severity

But the State loses money and here comes austerity

Collapsing economies are not met with popularity

So remember a phrase- you will see with clarity

"The government cannot tax you into prosperity"

B. CONSERVATIVE

B. CONSERVATIVE

But Billy on the other hand, got all the right chances

his government can't control everyone's finances

Billy can elect those who will protect his rights

Many have died for those freedoms, mostly in fights

Billy however, sees a threat off in the distance

Some hypocrites are chanting something about a "resistance"

Leftists say we don't want a government that's totalitarian

But put group identity first? Well, that's authoritarian

B. CONSERVATIVE

B. CONSERVATIVE

Some government is good, but don't let it get out of hand

"We the People" is what makes our country grand

Our flag represents FREEDOM, so get up and stand!

B. CONSERVATIVE

Made in the USA
Columbia, SC
21 December 2021